W9-BMU-558

ESTIMATION

Globe
Fearon

Upper Saddle River,
New Jersey

Executive Editor: Barbara Levadi
Editors: Bernice Golden, Lynn Kloss, Bob McIlwaine, Kirsten Richert, Tom Repensek
Production Manager: Penny Gibson
Production Editor: Walt Niedner
Interior Design: The Wheetley Company
Electronic Page Production: The Wheetley Company
Cover Design: Pat Smythe

Reviewers:

Elizabeth Marquez, B.A., M.A.
Mathematics Teacher
North Brunswick Township High School
North Brunswick, NJ

Elliott Ringhel
Assistant Principal for Mathematics
Prospect Heights High School
Brooklyn, NY

Printed in the United States of America   5 6 7 8 9 10 04 03 02 01

ISBN 0-8359-1558-1

CONTENTS

TO THE STUDENT

Access to Math is a series of 15 books designed to help you learn new skills and practice these skills in mathematics. You'll learn the steps necessary to solve a range of mathematical problems.

LESSONS HAVE THE FOLLOWING FEATURES:

❖ Lessons are easy to use. Many begin with a sample problem from a real-life experience. After the sample problem is introduced, you are taught step-by-step how to find the answer. Examples show you how to use your skills.

❖ The *Guided Practice* section demonstrates how to solve a problem similar to the sample problem. Answers are given in the first part of the problem to help you find the final answer.

❖ The *Exercises* section gives you the opportunity to practice the skill presented in the lesson.

❖ The *Application* section applies the math skill in a practical or real-life situation. You will learn how to put your knowledge into action by using manipulatives and calculators, and by working problems through with a partner or a group.

Each book ends with *Cumulative Reviews*. These reviews will help you determine if you have learned the skills in the previous lessons. The *Selected Answers* section at the end of each book lists answers to the odd-numbered exercises. Use the answers to check your work.

Working carefully through the exercises in this book will help you understand and appreciate math in your daily life. You'll also gain more confidence in your math skills.

KNOWING WHEN TO ESTIMATE

estimate: a number, close to an exact amount, that tells *about* how much or how many

Perhaps you have seen the movie or read the book *Around the World in Eighty Days*. Do you know how many miles it is around the world?

The answer, *about* 25,000 miles, is an **estimate**. Scientists tell us the *exact* distance around the world is 24,846.5 miles. To estimate the distance, you can round to the nearest ten thousand.

Sometimes an estimate is acceptable, but other times an exact amount is required.

Scientists need to know that the exact distance to the moon is 238,857 miles. Most people will remember the estimate 200,000 miles.

You can estimate that you spend *about* ten dollars at the store, but you need to know that you spent *exactly* $9.73 when counting the change you receive from the clerk.

Guided Practice

For each of the following, decide whether an estimate is sufficient or whether an exact amount is required.

1. Your class will receive one dollar for each ticket sold at a school concert.

   a. Is it necessary to count the tickets? _____*yes*_____

   b. Is an estimate sufficient or is an exact amount required? _____

2. You drove from your home to visit a relative who lives in another state. A friend asks about how long the trip took.

   a. Is it necessary to give the time to the nearest minute or can you round to the number of hours?

   _____

   b. Is an estimate sufficient or is an exact amount required? _____

Exercises

 For each situation below, tell whether an exact value or an estimate is more appropriate. Explain why. You may want to talk with a partner about whether you need an estimated value or an exact value.

3. the amount of change back from $20.00 for $16.89 worth of groceries

_____

4. the number of items answered correctly on a test

_____

5. the number of Spanish-speaking people in a city

_____

6. the amounts for a monthly personal budget

_____

7. the amount of a checkbook balance

_____

8. the time it takes to get to school

_____

Application

9. You are the owner of a catering service that provides food for parties, weddings, and other events. A politician wants you to cater a large banquet. Describe the information you need to plan the banquet. Tell whether you will use estimates or exact answers and explain why.

_____

_____

_____

ROUNDING WHOLE NUMBERS

Vocabulary

place value: the value of a digit determined by its position in a number

rounding: finding the value of a number to a particular place value

An automobile dealer sold 5,624 cars. When filling out a survey that asks the dealer to estimate to the nearest hundred the number of cars sold, she writes 5,600. How did the dealer estimate 5,600?

When exact values are not necessary, estimates can be made by **rounding** numbers. Rounding means finding the value of a number to a particular **place value**. This often makes it easier to work with numbers.

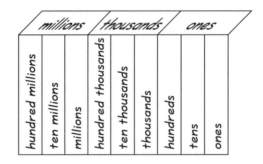

Reminder

A digit is any of the ten symbols 0 through 9.

To round a number to a particular place value, look at the digit in that place value. Then look at the first digit to the right. If the digit to the right is less than 5, the digit to be rounded does not change. If the digit to the right is 5 or more, the digit to be rounded is increased by one. After rounding, replace all the digits to the right of the rounded digit with zeros.

Round 5,624 to the nearest hundred.

5,	6	2	4
	6 is in the hundreds place	2 is the first digit to the right of the hundreds place	

Since 2 is less than 5, the 6 does not change.
Substitute zeros for 2 and 4.
5,624 is 5,600 when rounded to the nearest hundred.

Round 38,725 to the nearest thousand.

3	8,	7	2	5
	8 is in the thousands place	*7 is the first digit to the right of the thousands place*		

Because 7 is more than 5, add 1 to the digit in the thousands place.
8 becomes 9.
Substitute zeros for 7, 2, and 5.
38,725 is 39,000 when rounded to the nearest thousand.

Guided Practice

1. Round 863 to the nearest ten.

   a. What digit is in the tens place? _____6_____

   b. What digit is to the right of the tens place? _____3_____

   c. Is that digit less than, equal to, or more than 5? _____

   d. Substitute zeros for all digits after the tens place. _____

Exercises

Round each number below to the underlined place value.

2. 6̲73

3. 5̲42

4. 6,1̲22

_____

_____

_____

5. 16̲,725

6. 258̲,319

7. 56̲5,000

_____

_____

_____

Application

8. Describe a situation in which you might use estimation.

_____

_____

_____

MENTAL MATH WITH ADDITION AND SUBTRACTION OF WHOLE NUMBERS

Vocabulary

sum: the answer in addition

difference: the answer in subtraction

mental math: calculating an exact answer without using pencil and paper or a calculator

Adan and Isabel are cashiers for the snack stand at the community swimming pool. Adan uses a calculator to find the total for each buyer's purchases. Isabel finds the total in her head. Which method do you think is faster?

Add this column of purchases using a calculator. Then add the column without a calculator. Do you get the same total each time? Which way takes less time?

RECEIPT	
10 hot dogs	$20
chips	2
10 hamburgers	30
8 cones	12
8 apples	8
1 pair nose clips	1

Mental math means doing arithmetic in your head, without using pencil and paper or a calculator. You can use basic addition facts and some arithmetic rules to find **sums** or **differences** mentally.

Mental Math Tips for Addition

*   Look for numbers that add up to 10 or multiples of 10.

*   Make one number a multiple of 10. Subtract an amount from one number while adding the same amount to another number.

Mental Math Tip for Subtraction

*   Make the number you are subtracting a multiple of 10. Adding or subtracting the same amount from both numbers does not change the answer.

Reminder

When adding more than two numbers, you can combine them in any order to make easier sums.

Guided Practice

1. Use mental math to find the sum.

$$\begin{array}{r} 47 \\ 19 \\ + 23 \end{array} \quad \rightarrow \quad \begin{array}{r} 47 \\ 23 \\ + 19 \end{array}$$

   a. Which two numbers are now easy to add?
   47 and 23

   b. What is the sum of these two numbers?
   _70_

c. How might you find the total? _____

d. Find the total. _____

2. Use mental math to find the difference.

a. What value is added to both numbers? ___2___

$$\begin{array}{rcr} 121 & \to & 123 \\ -38 & \to & -40 \end{array}$$

b. Find the difference.

_____

Exercises

Use mental math to find each sum or difference. Use strategies so you can work faster than a calculator.

3. $9 + 5 + 1 =$ _____

4. $45 - 19 =$ _____

5. $17 + 23 + 60 =$ _____

6. $48 + 25 + 22 =$ _____

7. $102 - 68 =$ _____

8. $94 + 36 + 51 =$ _____

9. $278 - 46 =$ _____

10. $257 + 98 =$ _____

Application

Decide whether to use mental math or a calculator to solve this problem.

11. Lina works after school as a shipping clerk for Express Service. A client has a package that is 21 in. wide, 39 in. high, and 39 in. long. Express Service will not send a package if its combined width, height, and length is greater than 108 in.

a. Will Lina be able to mail the package by Express Service? _____

b. How do you know? _____

_____

c. Is an exact answer necessary? Why or why not?

_____

_____

ESTIMATING SUMS OF WHOLE NUMBERS

Ming, Josef, and Maria decided to combine their savings and buy a business that makes and sells T-shirts. The business will cost $70,000. Ming has $28,950 in savings, Josef has $23,125 in savings, and Maria has $34,095. Estimate to determine if they have enough combined savings to buy the business.

First, round each number to the nearest ten thousand because the purchase price is in the ten-thousands.

$28,950 rounds to $30,000

$23,125 rounds to $20,000

$34,095 rounds to $30,000

Reminder

The sum is the answer in addition.

Then, add the rounded numbers. The sum is $80,000, so Ming, Josef, and Maria have enough savings to purchase the business. By rounding, you are able to estimate the sum and answer the question without using a calculator or pencil and paper.

Guided Practice

Use the table below to answer the questions.

Busiest United States Ports (in tonnage)

Port	Imports	Exports
South Louisiana	25,859,022	63,262,655
Houston	41,065,418	27,225,217

1. Estimate the total import-export tonnage for the port of South Louisiana.

   a. Round the imports to the nearest ten million.
   _30,000,000_

   b. Round the exports to the nearest ten million.
   _60,000,000_

   c. Add the two rounded numbers. _____

2. Estimate the total import-export tonnage for the port of Houston.

    a. Round the imports to the nearest ten million.
    _____

    b. Round the exports to the nearest ten million.
    _____

    c. Add the two rounded numbers. _____

Exercises

Round each number to its greatest place value. Write the rounded number next to the exact value. Then estimate the sum using your rounded numbers.

3.   39 _____
       61 _____
    + 975 _____

4.   354 _____
    + 296 _____

5.   98 _____
   + 78 _____

6.   5,783 _____
   + 7,395 _____

7. 19,500 _____
   10,375 _____
  + 5,200 _____

8.   43,800 _____
  + 15,000 _____

9.   6,738 _____
   8,619 _____
   4,713 _____
  + 1,181 _____

10.   1,471 _____
    519 _____
    814 _____
  + 2,000 _____

11.   67,415 _____
   8,902 _____
  13,006 _____
  + 917 _____

Application

12. At an office supply store, Marco buys a package of computer diskettes for $3.99, a software manual for $10.99, a calendar refill for $4.95, and a battery-operated pencil sharpener for $8.29.

    a. About how much will he spend? _____

    b. About how much change should he receive from $40?

    _____

    c. If Marco found two software programs, one selling for $5.95 and the other for $6.95, could he buy both of them in addition to his other purchases? _____

ESTIMATING DIFFERENCES OF WHOLE NUMBERS

Estelle works for a company that manufactures portable voting booths. Part of her job is to keep track of population figures so her company will know where to move and store its equipment.

How can Estelle estimate the difference in population in New York City from 1960 to 1990?

Reminder

The difference is the answer in subtraction.

Population of Four Cities, 1960 – 1990

City	1960	1970	1980	1990
New York, NY	7,781,984	7,896,000	7,072,000	7,322,564
Los Angeles, CA	2,479,015	2,812,000	2,969,000	3,485,398
Chicago, IL	3,550,404	3,369,000	3,005,000	2,783,726
Houston, TX	938,219	1,234,000	1,595,000	1,630,672

Estelle does not need exact figures, so she rounds the numbers in the table. That makes the numbers easier to work with and easier to remember.

Population of New York City

Year	Population	Rounded to Hundred-Thousands
1960	7,781,984	7,800,000
1990	7,322,564	7,300,000

Then Estelle subtracts the rounded numbers. She uses mental math to subtract 7,300,000 from 7,800,000. The difference is 500,000. About 500,000 fewer persons lived in New York City in 1990 than in 1960.

Guided Practice

Use the table above to answer the following questions.

1. Estimate the difference in the population of Chicago, Illinois, between 1960 and 1990.

   a. Round the exact population to the nearest hundred thousand for 1960 and 1990.

Year	Population	Rounded to Hundred-Thousands
1960	3,550,404	3,600,000
1990	_____	_____

b. Use mental math to find the difference between the two rounded numbers. _____

Exercises

Round each number to the greatest place value. Write the rounded number next to the exact number. Then estimate the difference using the rounded numbers.

2.　　89 _____
　　− 42 _____

3.　1,025 _____
　− 690 _____

4.　7,345 _____
　− 5,980 _____

5.　2,066 _____
　− 792 _____

6.　9,440 _____
　− 7,350 _____

7.　46,840 _____
　− 25,075 _____

8. 86,250 _____
　− 53,400 _____

9. 725,500 _____
　− 28,954 _____

Choose the letter that is the best estimate for the difference.

10.　4,526 − 1,389 _____　　a.　60,000

11. 75,438 − 22,695 _____　　b.　4,000

12.　5,927 − 3,620 _____　　c.　2,000

Application

Use the table at the right to answer the following questions.

13. Estimate the difference between the number of cable subscribers in 1975 and the number of subscribers in 1990. _____

U.S. Households with Cable TV

Year	Subscribers
1975	9,596,690
1980	17,671,490
1985	39,872,520
1990	54,871,330

14. Estimate during which 5-year period the number of cable subscribers increased the most. _____

ESTIMATING AVERAGES

Vocabulary

addend: a number that is part of a sum

average: the sum of a set of numbers divided by the number of addends

data: facts or figures used to make conclusions

Otis works at the Tourist Bureau for a large city. He collects **data**, which are facts and figures, and he presents that information in tourist brochures. The table below shows prices of hotel rooms from a survey of five downtown hotels. For his brochure, Otis wants to estimate the **average** cost of a downtown hotel room.

Hotel	The Holiday Hotel	Dave's Inn	Charmaine Louise	The Local Inn	Hotel de Paris
Room Cost	$125	$198	$134	$98	$225

To estimate the average cost, Otis rounds each price to the nearest ten dollars. This gives him a list of **addends**, which he can add mentally.

	rounds to	
$125	→	$130
198	→	200
134	→	130
98	→	100
225	→	+ 230
		$790

Then Otis divides the sum by the number of prices.

$$\$790 \div 5 \; prices = \$158$$

The value $158 is the **average**. It represents a typical cost for a hotel room.

Guided Practice

1. The table below shows the number of sunny days during the peak tourist season in a city. Estimate the **average** number of sunny days per month.

Month	June	July	August
Number of Sunny Days	14	21	27

a. Round each number of sunny days to the tens place.

$14 \rightarrow \underline{\quad 10 \quad}$ $21 \rightarrow \underline{\quad 20 \quad}$ $27 \rightarrow \underline{\quad 30 \quad}$

b. Add the rounded number of days.

$\underline{\quad 10 \quad} + \underline{\quad 20 \quad} + \underline{\quad 30 \quad} = \underline{\qquad}$

c. Divide the sum by 3. $\underline{\qquad} \div 3 = \underline{\qquad}$

d. The average number of sunny days per month is

$\underline{\qquad\qquad}$.

Exercises

Estimate the average for each set of numbers.

2. 64, 72, 99, 13

3. 68, 83, 57

4. 18, 20, 22, 21

5. 522, 811, 785

6. 212, 187, 300, 481

7. 89, 34, 104, 96

8. 897, 602, 778, 96

9. 383, 632, 241

10. 78, 89, 68, 87, 69, 81

Application

Work with a partner.

11. The chart below shows the monthly attendance at a city zoo. Estimate the average monthly attendance for the year. Use a calculator to find an exact value for the average monthly attendance. Compare your estimated average to your calculated average.

Month	Attendance	Month	Attendance
Jan.	2,894	Jul.	47,694
Feb.	7,846	Aug.	30,406
Mar.	9,305	Sept.	29,421
Apr.	14,862	Oct.	15,694
May	19,426	Nov.	14,986
Jun.	37,861	Dec.	9,721

Estimated average _____   Exact average _____

ROUNDING DECIMALS

Vocabulary

decimal: a number that contains place values to the right of the ones place to show tenths, hundredths, thousandths, and so on.

Reminder

The value of a digit is determined by its position in the number.

Arlo has a weekend job at the dock of an exporter. The cargo containers there are measured in metric tons. Arlo multiplies by the factor 1.1023 to change metric tons to short tons.

hundred-thousands 100,000	ten-thousands 10,000	thousands 1,000	hundreds 100	tens 10	ones 1	tenths 0.1	hundredths 0.01	thousandths 0.001	ten-thousandths 0.0001	hundred-thousandths 0.00001
					1	1	0	2	3	

The place value chart shows the **decimal** 1.1023.

Sometimes Arlo rounds 1.1023 to the nearest tenth before using it. A rounded number is easier to work with and can be used to estimate answers that are close to the exact value.

To round a number to a particular place, look at the digit in that place value. When Arlo rounds to the nearest tenth, he looks at 1.1023.

Next, look at the first digit to the right. If the digit to the right is less than 5, the digit to be rounded remains the same. If the digit to the right is 5 or more, the digit to be rounded is increased by 1.

When rounding to the ones place or to any place to the right of the decimal point, all the digits to the right of the rounded digit can be dropped.

So, Arlo's estimate to the nearest tenth is 1.1.

When you round money amounts to the nearest tenth, or ten cents, instead of dropping all the digits to the right of the rounded digit, you add zero.

$57.78 ⟶ $57.80

Otherwise, treat money amounts as any other decimal.

$450.785 ⟶ $450.79

$83.41 ⟶ $83

1. Round 3.385 to the nearest hundredth.

   a. Underline the digit in the hundredths place.   3 . 3 __8__ 5

   b. Circle the digit to the right of the hundredths place. 3 . 3 8 5

   c. Is that digit greater than, equal to, or less than 5? _____

   d. Round 3.385 to the nearest hundredth. _____

2. Round $342.52 to the nearest tenth.

   a. Underline the digit in the tenths place. $342.52

   b. Circle the digit to the right of the tenths place. $342.52

   c. Is that digit greater than, equal to, or less than 5? _____

   d. Round $342.52 to the nearest tenth. _____

Exercises

Round each number to the underlined place value.

3. 78.089 _____

4. 213.946 _____

5. $14.61 _____

6. 0.13586 _____

7. $0.851 _____

8. $9.848 _____

9. $0.78 _____

10. 0.4196 _____

11. 2.15073 _____

Application

COOPERATIVE **Work with a partner. Round each decimal to the given place.**

LEARNING

12. A foot is exactly 0.3048 meter. Round this number to the nearest thousandth. _____

13. An inch is exactly 2.54 centimeters. Round this number to its **greatest** place value. _____

14. A degree of latitude is about 69.171 miles at the equator. **Round this** number to its greatest place value. _____

15. A micrometer is about 0.0000397 inch. Round this **number to the** nearest hundred-thousandth. _____

ESTIMATING SUMS OF DECIMALS

Radhika drives a car to work every day. She filled the tank with gasoline four times this month. The charges this month were $16.37, $17.59, $14.48, and $12.83. Radhika wants to estimate the total.

She estimates by rounding each amount to the nearest ten dollars and adding.

$$\begin{array}{rcl}
\$16.37 & \longrightarrow & \$20 \\
17.59 & \longrightarrow & 20 \\
14.48 & \longrightarrow & 10 \\
12.83 & \longrightarrow & +\ 10 \\
\hline
& & \$60
\end{array}$$

Reminder

To round a number, look at the digit to the right of the place you're rounding to. If that digit is less than 5, round down. If that digit is 5 or more, round up.

Radhika paid about $60 for gasoline this month.

Radhika decides she needs a closer estimate. She estimates by rounding each amount to the nearest ten cents (tenth) and adding.

$$\begin{array}{rcl}
\$16.37 & \longrightarrow & \$16.40 \\
17.59 & \longrightarrow & 17.60 \\
14.48 & \longrightarrow & 14.50 \\
12.83 & \longrightarrow & +\ 12.80 \\
\hline
& & \$61.30
\end{array}$$

Guided Practice

1. Radhika keeps track of the miles she drives. Here are the numbers of miles for a three-month period: 1,121.57; 952.14; 1,185.86. Estimate the total miles driven to the nearest mile.

   a. Round each number to the ones place.
      <u>1,122</u>   <u>952</u>   <u>1,186</u>

   b. Add the rounded numbers. Sum = _____

   c. The estimated number of miles driven is

      _____ .

Round to the tenths place. Estimate each sum.

2. 13.58 _____	**3.** 123.583 _____	**4.** 2,153.47 _____
67.41 _____	305.427 _____	+ 3,958.94 _____
+ 25.69 _____	+ 786.082 _____	

Round to the ones place. Estimate each sum.

5. 13.58 _____	**6.** 123.583 _____	**7.** 2,153.47 _____
67.41 _____	305.427 _____	+ 3,958.94 _____
+ 25.69 _____	+ 786.082 _____	

Round to the tens place. Estimate each sum.

8. 13.58 _____	**9.** 123.583 _____	**10.** 2,153.47 _____
67.41 _____	305.427 _____	+ 3,958.94 _____
+ 25.69 _____	+ 786.082 _____	

Application

COOPERATIVE LEARNING

11. Work with one or two other students. Each person should place a small handful of coins on the table. Reserve a few dimes and nickels to use for rounding.

First, each person should round his or her pile of coins to the nearest ten cents. If you are rounding up, use the dimes and nickels from the reserve pile to make up the rounded amount. To the nearest ten cents, how much money is in your pile of coins?

_____

Finally, add the amounts in the rounded piles. Do not count the coins left in the reserve pile, if any. How much money did your group have to the nearest ten cents?

_____

ESTIMATING SUMS OF ADDENDS

Mr. Marino gives a score for each activity and assignment in his math class. Margaret's scores during this marking period are 8, 23, 79, 91, 62, 41, 98, 22, 19, and 38. How can Margaret estimate her total score?

Here is one way to estimate Margaret's total score. First, round each score to the nearest ten. Then look for scores such as 10 + 90 that combine to make 100.

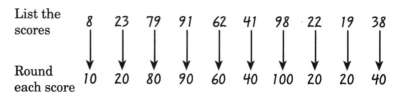

You can use brackets to mark each pair or group of scores that combine to make 100. Then you can mentally estimate the total.

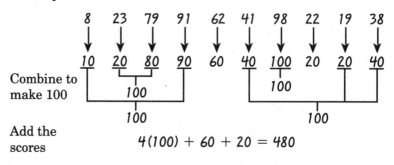

Margaret's estimated total score is 480.

Guided Practice

1. A gymnast's practice scores are 3.9, 4.3, 3.8, 4.7, 5.9, 6.3, 4.8, 5.2, and 6.2. She needs a total score of 45 to qualify for the Olympics. Estimate her total. Round each score to the nearest whole number.

   a. What is each rounded score? <u>4, 4, 4, 5, 6, 6, 5, 5, 6</u>

   b. Which groups of scores combine to make 10?

   _____

   c. What is the gymnast's estimated total score?

   _____

   d. Will she qualify for the Olympics? Explain.

   _____

Round each number to the greatest place value. Estimate each sum. Then use a calculator to find the exact sum.

2. 29, 48, 61, 77, 93, 31, 57, 88

Estimated sum: _____

Exact sum: _____

3. 4.1, 2.7, 7.3, 1.4, 8.8, 5.9, 3.2, 9.8

Estimated sum: _____

Exact sum: _____

4. 119, 911, 234, 476, 735, 987, 502, 345, 278

Estimated sum: _____

Exact sum: _____

5. 9.87, 3.75, 2.19, 7.75, 3.75, 2.17, 4.98, 6.05, 2.02, 8.88

Estimated sum: _____

Exact sum: _____

6. 37, 58, 79, 81, 24, 31, 98, 66, 45, 38, 12, 42

Estimated sum: _____

Exact sum: _____

7. 168, 342, 797, 656, 845, 174, 496, 543, 942, 109

Estimated sum: _____

Exact sum: _____

Application

8. Marco deposited the following baby-sitting payments into his savings account: $17, $23, $12, $21, $18, $9, $15, $18, $27, $19, and $12. Estimate how much money Marco deposited into his account.

_____

9. Write a list of ten numbers that have an estimated sum of 700.

_____

10. Describe your strategy for finding the numbers you listed in Application 9.

_____

_____

_____

_____

_____

_____

ESTIMATING DIFFERENCES OF DECIMALS

Roshie is buying a pair of jeans for $14.97. She is paying for them with a $20 bill. Will Roshie have enough money left to buy a T-shirt for $6.99?

Roshie estimates her change. She does not need an exact amount. She estimates by rounding to the nearest dollar and then subtracting.

$$\begin{array}{lcl} \$20.00 & \longrightarrow & \$20 \\ -\ 14.97 & \longrightarrow & -\ 15 \\ \hline & & \$5 \end{array}$$

Roshie will receive about $5 in change from the $20 bill. She will not have enough money to buy the T-shirt.

Guided Practice

1. Roshie is buying a folder for $.77. She is paying for it with a one-dollar bill. Estimate her change.

   a. Estimate $.77 to the nearest ten cents. $.80

   b. Is it easier to subtract $.77 from $1.00 or to subtract $.80 from $1.00?

   _____

   c. Roshie should receive about _____ in change.

2. An eraser costs $0.57. Roshie has three quarters. Estimate her change.

    a. Write three quarters in cents. Three quarters =

       _____

    b. Round three quarters to the nearest ten cents.

       _____

    c. Round $0.57 to the nearest ten cents. _____

    d. Subtract the two rounded values.

       _____ − _____ = _____

    e. Roshie should receive about _____ in change.

Exercises

Round each decimal to the nearest one. Estimate each difference.

3. 20.96 _____
   − 8.12 _____

4. 12.88 _____
   − 9.3 _____

5. 6.3 _____
   −0.98 _____

6. 19.057 _____
   − 4.32 _____

7. 32.79 _____
   − 13.19 _____

8. 70.00 _____
   − 19.752 _____

9. $39.00 _____
   − 28.97 _____

10. 9.632 _____
   − 5.444 _____

11. 12.89 _____
   − 5.24 _____

Application

 Use a calculator to solve each problem. Then use rounding and estimation to check your calculator answer.

12. During one winter 38.75 inches of snow fell in Washington, D.C. During the next winter only 12.23 inches of snow fell. About how much more snow fell the first year than the second year?

    Calculator answer: _____   Estimated answer: _____

13. Kristelle swam the 50-meter breaststroke in 60.89 seconds, and she swam the 50-meter freestyle in 54.93 seconds. About how much faster is Kristelle's freestyle than her breaststroke over 50 meters?

    Calculator answer: _____   Estimated answer: _____

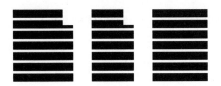

MENTAL MATH WITH PRODUCTS OF WHOLE NUMBERS

Vocabulary

factor: a number that is multiplied by other numbers

product: the answer in a multiplication problem

Gloria collects baseball cards. She keeps them in plastic sheets that display 18 cards (9 cards on each side). How many cards can she display on 20 sheets? You can use mental math to find the answer for 18×20.

First multiply the nonzero digits, then write as many zeros as there are in the **factors**.

18×20

$18 \times 2 = 36$ Multiply the nonzero digits.

$\qquad\quad = 360$ Add one zero.

Gloria can display 360 cards. The factors are 18 and 20. The **product** is 360.

Here are two rules that can be used to find a product mentally. Commutative Property of Multiplication: changing order of the factors does not change the product.

$$3 \times 4 = 4 \times 3 \qquad 18 \times 20 = 20 \times 18$$
$$12 = 12 \qquad\qquad 360 = 360$$

Associative Property of Multiplication: grouping factors differently does not change the product.

$$(2 \times 3) \times 4 = 2 \times (3 \times 4)$$
$$6 \times 4 = 2 \times 12$$
$$24 = 24$$

Gloria has 18 baseball cards displayed on 12 sheets. How many cards does she have displayed?

Think. $18 = 2 \times 9$

Multiply. $(2 \times 9) \times 12 = 2 \times (9 \times 12)$
$$= 2 \times 108$$
$$= 216$$

Gloria has 216 cards displayed.

1. Use mental math to multiply 400 × 80.

    a. Identify the nonzero digits. _4 and 8_

    b. Multiply these digits. _32_

    c. Count the zeros in the factors. _____

    d. Write the product. _____

2. Use mental math to multiply 5 × 7 × 6.

    a. What factors have a product that is a multiple of 10? _____

    b. Reorder the factors. _____

    c. Find the product. _____

Exercises

Use mental math to find each product.

3. 5 × 300

_____

4. 20 × 45

_____

5. 4 × 13 × 5

_____

6. 220 × 40

_____

7. 35 × 4

_____

8. 66 × 90

_____

9. 2 × 11 × 25

_____

10. 8 × 25

_____

11. 5 × 7 × 12

_____

Application

12. Hilldale Park District has four buses for a trip to the zoo. Each bus holds 54 students. Can 250 students go on the trip? Use mental math to explain your answer.

    _____

    _____

ESTIMATING PRODUCTS OF WHOLE NUMBERS

Vocabulary

overestimate: an estimated value that is greater than the exact value

underestimate: an estimated value that is less than the exact value

Reminder

The product is the answer in a multiplication problem.

Reminder

If the digit to the right of the digit to be rounded is 5 or more than 5, round up.

Reminder

If the digit to the right of the digit to be rounded is less than 5, round down.

Example 1

Dante's uncle owns his own taxi cab. Dante keeps a record of the taxi's expenses, which average $35 a day for gas, tolls, and other costs. In the month of January the taxi will be driven 27 days. About how much will expenses be in January?

Dante can estimate the product by rounding each factor to its greatest place value.

$$\begin{array}{ccc} \$35 & \longrightarrow & \$40 \\ \times\ 27 & \longrightarrow & \times\ 30 \\ \hline (\$945) & & \$1{,}200 \end{array}$$

Dante budgets about $1,200 for the expenses in January.

In the above example notice that both factors rounded *up*. When both factors round up, the estimate is an **overestimate**, or more than the exact value.

Example 2

Lauren drives a limousine. Her average amount for daily expenses is $104, and the limousine will be driven for 23 days in January. About how much will her expenses be?

$$\begin{array}{ccc} \$104 & \longrightarrow & \$100 \\ \times\ 23 & \longrightarrow & \times\ 20 \\ \hline (\$2{,}392) & & \$2{,}000 \end{array}$$

Lauren's expenses will be about $2,000 in January.

Notice that both factors rounded *down*. When both factors round down, the estimate is an **underestimate**, or less than the exact value.

If Lauren drives the limousine for 28 days in February, about how much will her expenses be?

When one factor rounds up and the other rounds down, the estimate is very close to the exact product.

$$\$104 \longrightarrow 100$$
$$\underline{\times\ 28} \longrightarrow \underline{\times\ 30}$$
$$(\$2,912) \qquad\qquad \$3,000$$

Lauren's expenses will be about $3,000 in February.

Guided Practice

1. A company estimates that each of its 113 temporary employees will work 55 days during the fall sales campaign. Estimate the total number of days worked by the temporary employees.

   a. Round each number to its greatest place. 113 → _100_ , 55 → _60_

   b. Multiply the rounded numbers. _____ × _____ = _____

   c. About how many days will be worked? _____

Exercises

Estimate each product.

2. 28 _____
   × 36 _____

3. 31 _____
   × 67 _____

4. 287 _____
   × 49 _____

5. 499 _____
   × 71 _____

Application

6. Marc has a budget of $850 for a company outing. He wants to buy $26 hockey tickets for 34 employees. Estimate the cost of the tickets. Is the estimate over, under, or very close to the exact cost? Why?

   _____

   _____

ESTIMATING QUOTIENTS OF WHOLE NUMBERS

Vocabulary

dividend: the number that is divided in division

divisor: the number by which the dividend is divided in division

quotient: the answer in division

compatible numbers: numbers that are easy to work with mentally

Gustavo is helping plan the parent-teacher meetings for his school. In the storeroom there is enough coffee for 1,650 servings. At each meeting, he makes about 35 cups of coffee. After about how many meetings will Gustavo have to order more coffee?

This is a division problem. The answer to a division problem is called a **quotient**. To estimate the quotient, round the **dividend** and the **divisor**. Then change the rounded numbers to **compatible numbers**, numbers that are easy to divide mentally.

$$\begin{array}{ccc} \text{Round each} & & \text{Find compatible} \\ \text{number.} & & \text{numbers and divide.} \end{array}$$

$$1{,}650 \div 35 \quad 1{,}700 \div 40 \quad 1{,}600 \div 40 = 40 \leftarrow \text{Estimate}$$

Gustavo must order more coffee after about 40 meetings.

Use multiplication to check division.

$$40 \times 40 = 1{,}600$$

Guided Practice

1. A 64-page workbook contains 1,936 exercises. About how many exercises are on each page of the workbook?

   a. Round the dividend and the divisor to the greatest place. ___2,000___ ÷ ___60___

   b. Find a pair of compatible numbers.

   _____ ÷ _____

   c. What is the estimated number of exercises on each page? _____

Round each number. Then use compatible numbers and estimate each quotient. Finally, use a calculator to find the exact quotients to the nearest tenth.

2. 305 ÷ 57

Estimate: _____

Exact: _____

3. 581 ÷ 72

Estimate: _____

Exact: _____

4. 470 ÷ 48

Estimate: _____

Exact: _____

5. 625 ÷ 27

Estimate: _____

Exact: _____

6. 4,903 ÷ 13

Estimate: _____

Exact: _____

7. 5,780 ÷ 74

Estimate: _____

Exact: _____

8. 2,650 ÷ 31

Estimate: _____

Exact: _____

9. 17,381 ÷ 64

Estimate: _____

Exact: _____

10. 24,875 ÷ 53

Estimate: _____

Exact: _____

Application

COOPERATIVE LEARNING

Work with a partner. One partner estimates each quotient. The other partner uses a calculator to find the exact quotient. Then both partners compare values for each quotient.

11. About 11,850 students take a city bus tour each year. Each bus holds 34 students. About how many bus loads of student tours are there each year?

_____

12. A regional library has 35,099 books on 1,035 shelves. About how many books are on each shelf?

_____

 ESTIMATING PRODUCTS
OF DECIMALS

Example 1

Jacob works on the school newspaper. For a story on the science department, he has a photo of a centipede. The actual length of the centipede is 0.27 inches. If the photo enlarges the centipede 35 times, about how long is the centipede in the photo?

To estimate the length of the centipede, round each factor to its greatest place and multiply mentally.

35	rounds up to	40
× 0.27	rounds up to	× 0.3
(9.45)		12.0

The centipede will be about 12 inches long in the photo.

Because both numbers round up, the estimate is an overestimate of the actual length in the photo.

Example 2

Jacob tries to find the product of 14.2 × 7.14 on a calculator and gets 1.01388. Is that product correct?

You can also use estimation to check the place of a decimal point in a product. Round each factor to its greatest place and multiply mentally.

14.2	rounds down to	10
×7.14	rounds up to	× 10
		100

The decimal 1.01388 is not close to 100. So 1.01388 is not correct. The numbers were entered incorrectly. The correct product is 101.388, which is closer to 100.

Reminder

When both factors round up, the estimate is an overestimate. When both factors round down, the estimate is an underestimate.

Reminder

A product is the answer to a multiplication problem.

Guided Practice

1. Suppose a dragonfly is 0.76 inches long. If a magnifying glass enlarges the dragonfly 15 times, about how long will the dragonfly appear to be?

a. Round each factor to its greatest place.

0.76 rounds to ___0.8___.

15 rounds to _____.

b. Use mental math to find the product.

_____ × _____ = _____

c. The dragonfly will appear to be about

_____ inches long.

Exercises

Estimate each product.

2. 3.7 × 8.3   Rounded numbers: _____ × _____

Estimate: _____

3. 6.47 × 7.19   Rounded numbers: _____ × _____

Estimate: _____

4. 71.97 × 8   Rounded numbers: _____ × _____

Estimate: _____

5. 34.98 × 7.28   Rounded numbers: _____ × _____

Estimate: _____

6. 61.07 × 4.98   Rounded numbers: _____ × _____

Estimate: _____

Application

 For the exercise below, did the student enter the numbers correctly on the calculator? Estimate to tell why or why not.

7. Maria wants to find the product of 12.9 × 5.78. The calculator displays 745.62.

_____

_____

_____

15 ESTIMATING QUOTIENTS OF DECIMALS AND WHOLE NUMBERS

Lida is opening a used car lot. At one lot, the display area is 118.2 meters wide. If each car's space is 3 meters wide, how many cars can be displayed?

To estimate the quotient, round the decimal to its greatest place and find compatible numbers to divide.

	Round the decimal.	Find compatible numbers and divide.
$118.2 \div 3$	$100 \div 3$	$120 \div 3 = 40$

About 40 cars can be displayed in the lot.

Guided Practice

1. Hiroko works 12 hours a week and earns $78.60. About how much does she earn an hour?

   a. Write a division equation to solve.

   $\$78.60 \div 12 = ?$ _____

   b. Round the decimal.

   _____ ÷ _____

   c. Find compatible numbers to divide.

   _____ ÷ _____

   d. What is Hiroko's estimated hourly wage?

   _____

Use compatible numbers to estimate each quotient.

2. $83.6 \div 4$

3. $478.3 \div 6$

4. $724.63 \div 8$

5. $265.98 \div 3$

6. $148.625 \div 32$

7. $3{,}224.7 \div 8$

8. $3{,}559.34 \div 58$

9. $5{,}367.14 \div 91$

10. $559.827 \div 78$

Application

11. The winning time for four students running in a 400-meter relay race was 45.19 seconds.

a. Estimate the average time of each runner. _____

b. Explain how you got your answer.

12. Pens cost $3.45 a dozen.

a. Estimate the cost of one pen. _____

b. Explain how you got your answer.

13. A company buys 18 large cartons of paper. The bill is $714.25.

a. Estimate the cost of each carton. _____

b. Explain how you got your answer.

ESTIMATING SUMS OF FRACTIONS

Vocabulary

fraction: a number that names part of a whole or part of a set

Marie is making a centerpiece for a school dance. She has ribbon scraps that are $\frac{1}{4}$ yard, $\frac{3}{8}$ yard, and $\frac{5}{6}$ yard long. About how many yards of ribbon does Marie have?

To estimate the sum of **fractions**, round each fraction to the nearest half unit. Fractions less than $\frac{1}{4}$ round down to zero and fractions greater than or equal to $\frac{3}{4}$ round up to 1. Fractions between $\frac{1}{4}$ and $\frac{3}{4}$ round to $\frac{1}{2}$.

Actual lengths	Rounded lengths	Estimated sum
$\frac{1}{4} + \frac{3}{8} + \frac{5}{6}$	$0 + \frac{1}{2} + 1$	$1\frac{1}{2}$

Marie has about $1\frac{1}{2}$ yards of ribbon. You can use a calculator to check.

$$\frac{1}{4} = 0.250$$
$$\frac{3}{8} = 0.375$$
$$\frac{5}{6} = \underline{0.833}$$
$$1.458$$

1.458 is about $1\frac{1}{2}$, so Marie's estimate is reasonable.

Reminder

To change a fraction to a decimal, divide the numerator by the denominator.

Guided Practice

1. A broom handle is $\frac{4}{9}$ yard long, and it comes with an extension that is another $\frac{11}{18}$ yard. About how long is the handle with its extension?

   a. Round the addends. ____$\frac{1}{2}$____ + ____$\frac{1}{2}$____

   b. Add to estimate the sum. _____

   c. What is the actual length of the broom handle with its extra piece? _____

   d. Is your estimate reasonable? Explain.

   _____

   _____

Exercises

Round each fraction to the nearest half. Then use the rounded values to estimate the sum. You can use a calculator to check whether your estimate is reasonable.

2. $\dfrac{7}{8} + \dfrac{1}{3}$

Estimate: _____

3. $\dfrac{1}{7} + \dfrac{9}{12}$

Estimate: _____

4. $\dfrac{3}{8} + \dfrac{3}{4}$

Estimate: _____

5. $\dfrac{4}{7} + \dfrac{3}{15} + \dfrac{9}{10}$

Estimate: _____

6. $\dfrac{1}{6} + \dfrac{5}{8}$

Estimate: _____

7. $\dfrac{5}{6} + \dfrac{8}{9} + \dfrac{1}{12}$

Estimate: _____

8. $\dfrac{4}{5} + \dfrac{4}{9} + \dfrac{4}{25}$

Estimate: _____

9. $\dfrac{6}{7} + \dfrac{1}{9} + \dfrac{9}{10}$

Estimate: _____

10. $\dfrac{3}{5} + \dfrac{11}{12} + \dfrac{1}{8}$

Estimate: _____

Application

11. Draw 24 boxes like this.

These boxes represent the number of hours in a day.

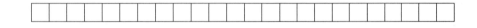

a. During a normal weekday (Monday through Friday), how many hours do you sleep? Fill in a box for each hour.

b. Draw 24 more boxes. Then fill in a box for each hour you spend in school.

c. Draw 24 more boxes. Fill in a box for each hour you spend doing chores, homework, or at an after-school job.

d. For each answer, use a fraction to show the number of shaded boxes divided by the total number of boxes. Then estimate the sum of your three fractions.

e. What does your answer to *d*, above, represent?

_____

_____

ESTIMATING SUMS OF MIXED NUMBERS

Vocabulary

mixed number: a number with a whole number and a fraction part

For a party, Manny made a vegetable salad with $3\frac{6}{7}$ pounds of tomatoes, $1\frac{3}{8}$ pounds of green peppers, $4\frac{1}{8}$ pounds of cucumbers, and $\frac{3}{7}$ pound of onions. About how many pounds of vegetables did Manny use in his salad?

The ingredients for Manny's salad are given as **mixed numbers**, with a whole number part and a fraction part. To estimate the sum of mixed numbers, round each fraction part to the nearest half unit.

$$3\frac{6}{7} + 1\frac{3}{8} + 4\frac{1}{8} + \frac{3}{7}$$

Rounded values   Estimated sum

$$4 + 1\frac{1}{2} + 4 + \frac{1}{2} \qquad\qquad 10$$

Manny used about 10 pounds of vegetables in his salad.

Guided Practice

1. A rectangular garden is $6\frac{3}{16}$ feet long and $4\frac{3}{4}$ feet wide. About how much fencing is needed to enclose the garden?

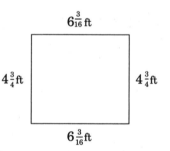

Reminder

To round to the nearest half unit, fraction parts equal to or less than $\frac{1}{4}$ round down to the whole number, and fraction parts equal to or greater than $\frac{3}{4}$ round up to the next whole number. Fractions between $\frac{1}{4}$ and $\frac{3}{4}$ round to $\frac{1}{2}$.

a. Round the length of the garden to the nearest half unit. _____6 ft_____

b. Round the width of the garden to the nearest half unit. _____

c. Add the rounded values of the four sides to estimate the sum.

_____

d. What is the actual amount of fencing needed?

_____

e. Is your estimate reasonable? Explain.

_____

_____

Exercises

Estimate each sum of mixed numbers by rounding the fractions to the nearest half unit.

2. $4 \frac{9}{10} + 3 \frac{1}{8}$

Estimate: _____

3. $3 \frac{1}{2} + 5 \frac{1}{10} + 9 \frac{1}{3}$

Estimate: _____

4. $6 \frac{1}{5} + 3 \frac{5}{6} + 9 \frac{1}{10}$

Estimate: _____

5. $6 \frac{1}{12} + 3 \frac{4}{5} + 9 \frac{1}{6} + 2 \frac{5}{9}$

Estimate: _____

6. $8 \frac{5}{6} + 10 \frac{2}{3} + 4 \frac{5}{24}$

Estimate: _____

7. $5 \frac{1}{20} + 6 \frac{1}{10} + 7 \frac{7}{8} + 2 \frac{3}{4}$

Estimate: _____

Application

COOPERATIVE LEARNING

Work with a partner to solve this problem.

8. The distance around this rectangle is 12 meters. The length and the width of the rectangle are mixed numbers.

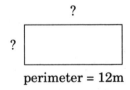

perimeter = 12m

a. Use estimation skills to find a possible length and width for the rectangle.

_____

b. Find another possible length and width for the rectangle.

_____

ESTIMATING DIFFERENCES OF FRACTIONS AND MIXED NUMBERS

Manuel makes jewelry to sell at an art fair. It takes $4\frac{1}{5}$ hours to make a bracelet and $6\frac{9}{10}$ hours to make a necklace. About how much longer does it take to make a necklace than a bracelet?

To estimate the difference between mixed numbers, round each fraction to the nearest half unit.

	Rounded values	Estimated difference
$6\frac{9}{10} - 4\frac{1}{5}$	$7 - 4$	3

It takes about 3 hours longer to make a necklace.

You can use a calculator to check whether your estimate is reasonable.

$$6\frac{9}{10} \qquad 6.9$$
$$-\ 4\frac{1}{5} \qquad -\ 4.2$$
$$\overline{\qquad} \qquad \overline{2.7}$$

The decimal 2.7 is the same as the mixed number $2\frac{7}{10}$. It takes exactly $2\frac{7}{10}$ hours longer to make a necklace than to make a bracelet. Manuel's estimate of 3 hours is reasonable.

Guided Practice

1. A small package of wire weighs $13\frac{5}{8}$ ounces. A large package of wire weighs $27\frac{1}{12}$ ounces. About how much more does a large package weigh than a small one?

   a. Round each mixed number. $\underline{\quad 13\frac{1}{2}\ oz \quad}$

   $\underline{27oz}$

Reminder

When finding the difference between two mixed numbers or between a whole number and a mixed number, regrouping may be necessary. $6 - 2\frac{3}{4} =$ $5\frac{4}{4} - 2\frac{3}{4} = 3\frac{1}{4}$

b. Write a subtraction equation to find the estimated difference.

_____

c. Rewrite the equation to show the regrouping needed to subtract.

_____

d. What is the estimated difference? _____

e. What is the exact difference? _____

f. Is your estimate reasonable? Explain.

_____

Exercises

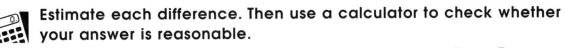

Estimate each difference. Then use a calculator to check whether your answer is reasonable.

2. $\frac{9}{10} - \frac{1}{2}$

Estimate: _____

3. $6\frac{5}{8} - 5\frac{1}{12}$

Estimate: _____

4. $9\frac{5}{9} - 7\frac{7}{9}$

Estimate: _____

5. $11\frac{9}{16} - \frac{7}{8}$

Estimate: _____

6. $3\frac{1}{12} - 1\frac{5}{12}$

Estimate: _____

7. $8\frac{3}{5} - 7\frac{9}{10}$

Estimate: _____

Application

COOPERATIVE LEARNING

8. Work with a partner. Start with a mixture of about 50 large paper clips and 15 small paper clips.

a. Take a small handful of your mixture. Then write the following two fractions:

$\dfrac{\text{number of large clips}}{\text{total number in handful}}$ 　　 $\dfrac{\text{number of small clips}}{\text{total number in handful}}$

b. Estimate the difference between the two fractions. _____

c. Mix all the paper clips together, and repeat steps a and b. Do this six times.

d. In step a, can you ever get a fraction that is equal to 1? Can you get a fraction that is greater than 1? Explain.

_____

9 ESTIMATING PRODUCTS OF FRACTIONS AND MIXED NUMBERS

Delinda does a report for her World Studies class. Her report is $8\frac{1}{4}$ handwritten pages, and Delinda can type a page in $5\frac{1}{2}$ minutes. She wants to know about how long it will take her to type the entire report.

The answer is the product of $8\frac{1}{4} \times 5\frac{1}{2}$. Delinda estimates this product by rounding each mixed number to the nearest whole number and multiplying.

Reminder

If the fraction part of a mixed number is less than $\frac{1}{2}$, round down. If it is greater than or equal to $\frac{1}{2}$, round up.

$$8\frac{1}{4} \quad \times \quad 5\frac{1}{2}$$
$$\downarrow \qquad\qquad \downarrow$$

Estimate: $\qquad 8 \quad \times \quad 6 \ = 48$

It will take Delinda about 48 minutes to type the report.

Guided Practice

1. Roberta travels $\frac{1}{2}$ mile to basketball practice each day. Helena travels $1\frac{2}{3}$ times as far as Roberta to get to practice. About how far does Helena travel to get to basketball practice?

   a. Write a multiplication problem. $\underline{\quad \frac{1}{2} \times 1\frac{2}{3} \quad}$

   b. Round the mixed number to the nearest whole number. _____

   c. Write the estimated product. _____

   d. Find the actual product. _____

   e. Compare. Is the estimate close to the actual product? _____

Reminder

To multiply mixed numbers, change them to fractions and multiply.

Estimate each product. Then find the actual product.

2. $3\frac{1}{4} \times 4\frac{7}{8}$

Estimate: _____

Actual: _____

3. $\frac{1}{4} \times 2\frac{1}{3}$

Estimate: _____

Actual: _____

4. $3\frac{1}{3} \times 5\frac{1}{4}$

Estimate: _____

Actual: _____

Estimate each product.

5. $5\frac{2}{3} \times 1\frac{1}{5}$

_____

6. $\frac{7}{8} \times 7\frac{3}{7}$

_____

7. $6\frac{1}{4} \times 3\frac{3}{5}$

_____

8. $1\frac{7}{8} \times 4\frac{2}{3}$

_____

9. $9\frac{3}{8} \times 4\frac{4}{5}$

_____

10. $5\frac{6}{7} \times \frac{1}{8}$

_____

Application

11. Explain how you can estimate the product of $8\frac{1}{4} \times \frac{1}{2}$.

_____

_____

_____

12. Is the product of a mixed number and a fraction always less than the mixed number? Write a few sentences to tell why.

_____

_____

_____

ESTIMATING AREAS

Vocabulary

area: the number of square units that cover a figure

grid: a pattern of evenly spaced vertical and horizontal lines

Hattie works for her family's landscaping business. She uses a grid to plan a yard with a lawn and a flower bed. The **grid** below shows a client's oddly shaped lawn. How large is the lawn?

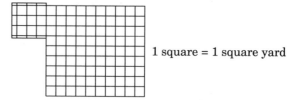

1 square = 1 square yard

Hattie needs to estimate the **area** of the lawn, which is the number of square units that cover the lawn. She begins with the rectangle and counts the number of small squares along the length (10) and along the width (9).

The formula for the area of a rectangle is
Area = length × width ($A = l \times w$).

Then Hattie uses the formula and rounds values to estimate the area.

$$A = l \times w$$
$$= 10 \times 10 = 100 \text{ square units}$$

Next, she counts the number of small squares along the length $\left(3\frac{1}{2}\right)$ and width $\left(3\frac{1}{2}\right)$ of the square figure.

The formula for the area of a square is
Area = side × side ($A = s \times s$).

Hattie uses the formula and rounded values to estimate the area.

$$A = s \times s$$
$$= 4 \times 4 = 16 \text{ square units}$$

Now she adds the two estimates to estimate the total area of the lawn.

$$100 + 16 = 116 \text{ square units}$$

Since each square on the grid represents one square yard, the area of the lawn is about 116 square yards.

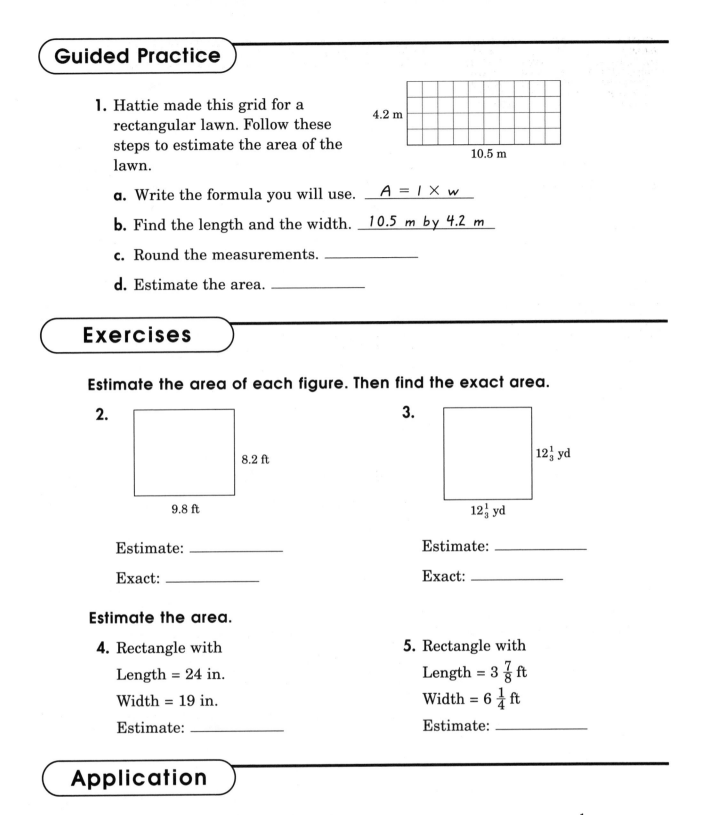

Guided Practice

1. Hattie made this grid for a rectangular lawn. Follow these steps to estimate the area of the lawn.

   4.2 m

   10.5 m

   a. Write the formula you will use. $\underline{A = l \times w}$

   b. Find the length and the width. $\underline{10.5 \text{ m by } 4.2 \text{ m}}$

   c. Round the measurements. _____

   d. Estimate the area. _____

Exercises

Estimate the area of each figure. Then find the exact area.

2.

   8.2 ft

   9.8 ft

   Estimate: _____

   Exact: _____

3.

   $12\frac{1}{3}$ yd

   $12\frac{1}{3}$ yd

   Estimate: _____

   Exact: _____

Estimate the area.

4. Rectangle with

   Length = 24 in.

   Width = 19 in.

   Estimate: _____

5. Rectangle with

   Length = $3\frac{7}{8}$ ft

   Width = $6\frac{1}{4}$ ft

   Estimate: _____

Application

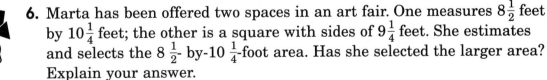

6. Marta has been offered two spaces in an art fair. One measures $8\frac{1}{2}$ feet by $10\frac{1}{4}$ feet; the other is a square with sides of $9\frac{1}{4}$ feet. She estimates and selects the $8\frac{1}{2}$- by-$10\frac{1}{4}$-foot area. Has she selected the larger area? Explain your answer.

   _____

   _____

ESTIMATING AREAS OF IRREGULAR FIGURES

Carmina is making a poster for her American History class. On the poster, she wants to estimate the area of Arizona. To estimate the area, Carmina draws a rectangle around an outline of the state.

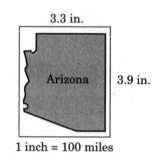

3.3 in.

Arizona   3.9 in.

1 inch = 100 miles

The rectangle is about 3 inches wide and 4 inches long. To estimate the area of Arizona in miles, Carmina uses the scale, which shows that 1 inch equals 100 miles.

Scale drawing   *Actual size*

3 in. by 4 in.   *300 mi by 400 mi*

$$Area = length \times width$$
$$= 300 \times 400$$
$$= 120,000 \; square \; miles$$

Carmina's estimate for the area of Arizona is about 120,000 square miles. Her teacher told her this was a reasonable estimate because Arizona's actual area is 114,000 square miles.

Reminder

You can use figures and formulas from geometry to estimate the area of an irregular shape.

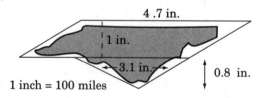

Guided Practice

1. Estimate the area of North Carolina.

4 .7 in.

1 in.

3.1 in.

0.8 in.

1 inch = 100 miles

a. What two shapes can be combined to represent North Carolina's irregular shape?

parallelogram _____

b. What is the estimated area (in square miles) of the parallelogram? Use the formula $A = b \times h$.

_____

c. What is the estimated area (in square miles) of the triangle? Use the formula $A = \frac{1}{2} \times (b \times h)$.

_____

d. What is the estimated area of North Carolina?

_____

Estimate the area of these irregular shapes.

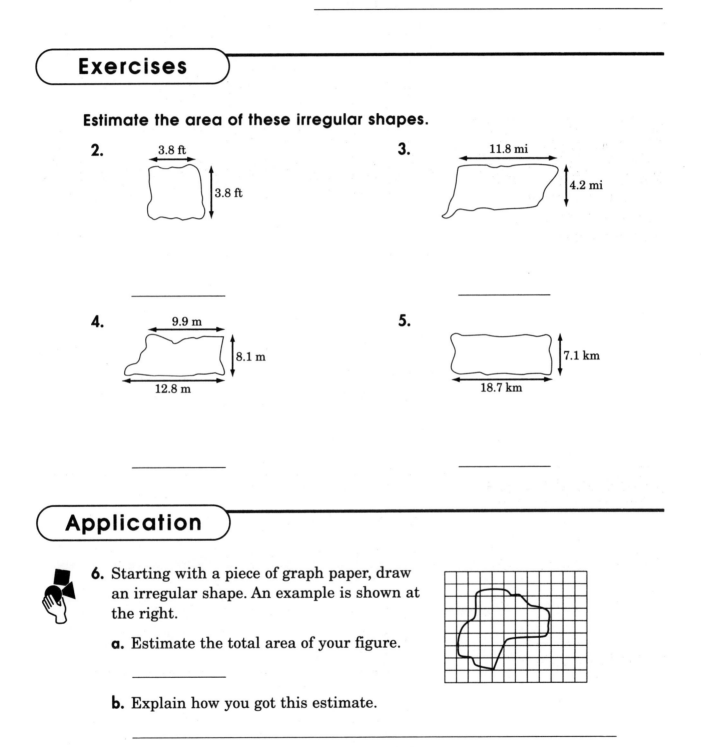

2. 3.8 ft

3.8 ft

_____

3. 11.8 mi

4.2 mi

_____

4. 9.9 m

8.1 m

12.8 m

_____

5. 7.1 km

18.7 km

_____

Application

6. Starting with a piece of graph paper, draw an irregular shape. An example is shown at the right.

a. Estimate the total area of your figure.

_____

b. Explain how you got this estimate.

_____

ESTIMATING PERCENTS

percent: a ratio that compares a number to 100; percent means "per hundred"

Mr. Devereaux looked at a sketch of the Miller's family room to see where their new rug should be placed. About what percent of the floor will be covered by the rug?

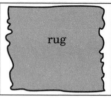

A **percent** is a ratio that compares a number to 100. To estimate the percent of the floor covered by the rug, divide the rectangle into equal parts so that the number of parts is a factor of 100. Below, the rectangle is divided into 20 equal parts.

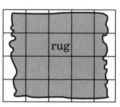

About 16 of the 20 equal parts will be covered by the rug.

$$\frac{16}{20} = \frac{(16 \times 5)}{(20 \times 5)} = \frac{80}{100} = 80\%$$

About 80% of the room will be covered by the rug.

Guided Practice

1. Darlene's circle graph shows how she spends her time each day. Estimate the percent of time Darlene spends at school.

Darlene's Day

   a. The broken lines divide the circle into __4__ equal parts.

   b. What fraction of the whole is represented by the section labeled "school"? _____

   c. What percent of the circle is this? _____

Exercises

Estimate what percent of each figure is shaded. Remember to divide the figure into equal parts, using a factor of 100 for the number of parts.

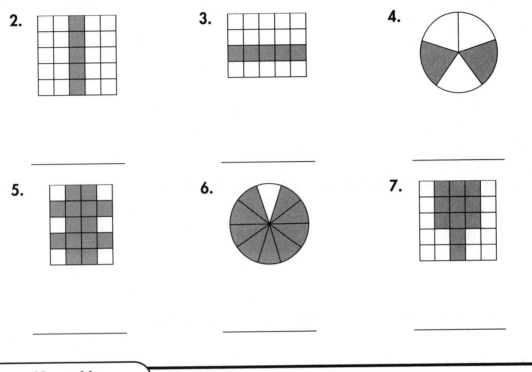

2. _____

3. _____

4. _____

5. _____

6. _____

7. _____

Application

8. Make your own circle graph of how you spend all the hours on a school day or weekend day. Make a list of your usual activities. Estimate what percent of time you spend doing each activity.

9. Describe what your circle graph shows.

_____

_____

_____

ESTIMATING THE PERCENT OF A NUMBER

Vocabulary

unit fraction: a fraction with a numerator of 1

At Wootton High School, 195 students play varsity sports and about 24% of these athletes are girls. About how many girls play varsity sports?

This problem can be put into a mathematical sentence.

$$24\% \text{ of } 195 = ?$$

The word "of" stands for multiplication, so the sentence can be rewritten.

$$24\% \times 195 = ?$$

Reminder

$10\% = \frac{1}{10}$ $20\% = \frac{1}{5}$

$25\% = \frac{1}{4}$ $33\frac{1}{3}\% = \frac{1}{3}$

$50\% = \frac{1}{2}$

To estimate the percent of a number, you can replace the percent with a fraction and replace the number with a rounded value. When you replace the percent, use a **unit fraction**, which is a fraction with a numerator of 1.

24% is close to 25%. $25\% = \frac{1}{4}$

195 rounds to 200. 200

Estimate. $\frac{1}{4} \times 200 = 50$

About 50 girls play varsity sports.

You can use a calculator percent key to find the exact answer.

Press: **1** **9** **5** **x** **2** **4** **%**
Display: **4** **6** **.** **8**

Guided Practice

1. About 11% of the 195 students in varsity sports play tennis. About how many students play tennis?

   a. Write a multiplication sentence that shows this problem.

b. Replace the percent with a unit fraction. $\frac{1}{10}$

c. Round the number of students who play varsity sports. _____

d. Estimate how many students play tennis.

_____

e. Use a calculator to find the actual number of students who play tennis. Is your estimate close?

_____

Exercises

Estimate each product by replacing the percent with a unit fraction and replacing the number with a rounded value.

2. 53% of 180

_____

3. 23% of 95

_____

4. 19% of 285

_____

5. 52% of 49

_____

6. 21% of 410

_____

7. 35% of 60

_____

Application

COOPERATIVE LEARNING

Work with a partner to solve these problems.

8. Ms. Garcia is driving to New York from Washington, D.C. She has completed about 52% of the 210-mile trip. Estimate how many miles Ms. Garcia has driven.

_____

9. About 34% of the 585 students enrolled in Fuji's Karate School achieve black belt status. Estimate how many of Fuji's students earn black belts.

_____

10. Is each estimate in Applications 8 and 9 an underestimate, an overestimate, or a very close estimate? Explain your reasoning.

_____

_____

 **ESTIMATING THE RATE**

A healthy body contains a lot of water! For every 9 pounds of your weight, about 6 pounds are water. About what percent of your body weight is water?

To estimate the percent of your weight that is water, start with the ratio that 6 out of 9 pounds of body weight is water. Then find an equivalent fraction with a denominator of 100. Write that fraction as a percent.

Reminder

Percent means "per hundred."

$$\frac{6}{9} \text{ is close to } \frac{6}{10}$$

$$\frac{6}{10} \times \frac{10}{10} = \frac{60}{100} = 60\%$$

About 60% of your body weight is water.

Guided Practice

1. In a recent survey at Cabin High School, it was reported that 19 out of 49 students spend more than one hour per night on homework. Estimate the percent of students who spend more than one hour per night on homework.

   a. Write a ratio comparing the number of students who spend more than one hour on homework to the number of students in the survey.
   $$\frac{19}{49}$$

   b. Round the numbers in the ratio. Your new denominator should be a factor of 100.
   $$\frac{20}{50}$$

   c. Write an equivalent fraction with denominator 100. _____

   d. Write the fraction as a percent. _____

   e. Use a calculator to find the exact percent. Divide $\frac{19}{49}$. Is your estimate close?

   _____

Exercises

Estimate the percent for each ratio.

2. 9 out of 10

_____

3. 24 out of 96

_____

4. 39 out of 48

_____

5. 4 out of 6

_____

6. 15 out of 21

_____

7. 21 out of 40

_____

8. 79 out of 187

_____

9. 23 out of 84

_____

10. 58 out of 97

_____

Application

COOPERATIVE LEARNING **Work with a partner to solve these problems.**

11. A typical fast-food hamburger weighs about 82 grams and has about 19 grams of fat. About what percent of the hamburger is fat?

_____

12. Public transportation officials in a large city found that 16 out of every 25 people like indoor mass transit train stations more than outdoor stations.

a. Estimate the percent of people who want to be inside.

_____

b. Estimate the percent of people who want to be outside.

_____

 **ESTIMATING COSTS OF TRIPS**

Example 1

Each January, the Patels drive 379 miles from their home in San Francisco to the Rose Bowl in Los Angeles. They spend $1.39 a gallon for gas, and their car gets about 21 miles to the gallon. About how much do they spend for gas for the one-way trip?

To estimate the number of gallons of gasoline they use, round the number of miles driven and the number of miles per gallon.

$$Number\ of\ gallons$$

$$= \frac{number\ of\ miles\ driven}{number\ of\ miles\ per\ gallon}$$

$$= \frac{379}{21} = \frac{400}{20} = 20\ gallons$$

To estimate the cost of the gasoline, use the rounded value for the number of gallons and round the cost per gallon.

$$Cost\ of\ gasoline$$

$$= number\ of\ gallons \times cost\ per\ gallon$$

$$= 20 \times \$1.39 = 20 \times \$1.50 = \$30$$

The Patels spend about $30 for gas for their one-way trip.

Example 2

Suppose the Patels want to estimate the total gasoline cost for the trip from San Francisco to Los Angeles, then back to San Francisco.

To find the round-trip cost, multiply the one-way estimate by two.

$$\$30 \times 2 = \$60$$

The Patels spend about $60 in gasoline for the round trip.

Guided Practice

1. Cheryl takes the subway to and from work each day at a round-trip cost of $4.80. Neil spends about $15.25 on gasoline each week, plus $3.90 per day for parking. Who spends less to and from work?

   a. About how much does Cheryl spend per day for the subway? Round to the nearest dollar. _____$5_____

   b. About how much does Neil spend per day for gasoline?

   _____ ÷ 5 = _____

   c. About how much does Neil spend daily on gas and parking?

   _____

   d. Who spends less daily, Cheryl or Neil? Explain.

   _____

   e. Why is it necessary to find Neil's daily gasoline cost?

   _____

Exercises

Estimate the following costs.

2. Find the mileage expense if you drive 589 miles at a cost of $0.21 per mile.

   Estimate: _____

3. Find the fare cost, if you get a discount of 19.96% off a fare of $100.

   Estimate: _____

Application

COOPERATIVE
LEARNING

4. Work with a partner to plan a trip and estimate the cost of the trip. Name your destination and record your estimates.

   _____

   _____

1. Tell whether the situations require an exact number or an estimation.

   a. the amount of ketchup on a hotdog _____

   b. the number of minutes left in a sports game _____

2. Raj likes to listen to the radio, but he doesn't like to listen to the same kind of music for a long time. Use the chart below to answer the following questions.

	Monday	Tuesday
8:00 A.M.	jazz	classical
8:25 A.M.	rock	rap
8:45 A.M.	jazz	country
9:15 A.M.	rap	jazz
9:30 A.M.	country	rock
10:15 A.M.	reggae	reggae

   a. Use mental math to add the number of minutes Raj listened to rap on Monday and Tuesday. Do the same for rock.

   Monday rap _____   Tuesday rap _____

   rock _____   rock _____

   b. Use mental math to find the difference between the number of minutes Raj listened to country music on Monday and Tuesday.

   _____

   c. Use mental math to find the difference between the number of minutes Raj listened to jazz on Monday and Tuesday.

   _____

3. Segal cooks a Middle Eastern dinner for her family. Her older brother is on a diet. He eats 965 calories for dinner. Segal prepares a bowl of chickpea hummus that is 210 calories per serving, falafel in a pita with yogurt dressing that is 725 calories per serving, and coffee that is 120 calories per cup.

   a. Estimate the number of calories in this meal. _____

   b. Estimate the difference between the number of calories Segal's brother is allowed and the calories in one serving of Segal's meal. Then find the exact answer.

   Estimate _____   Exact answer _____

4-6   CUMULATIVE REVIEW

1. Esther wants to be a doctor. She wonders how much she will spend during her first year of medical school. Her tuition is $22,600, her room and board is $8,200, and her books are $540. Round the three figures to their highest place value. Then add the figures. About how much will Esther spend during her first year of medical school? _____

2. Yancha cooks samosa pastries for her brothers. One cookbook tells her to cook the pastries at 425°, another says 375°, and one insists on 300°. Yancha averages the temperatures to make the perfect samosa. At about what degree does Yancha cook the samosas? _____

3. Gabriel and his friends shoot hoops with a neighborhood team. Use mental math to determine the average score for each quarter.

Score During Game	Gabriel's Team	Other Team	Average Score
1st quarter	14	10	_____
2nd quarter	22	29	_____
3rd quarter	44	46	_____
4th quarter	59	58	_____

4. Penny and Dolla shopped for a friend's birthday gift. Penny found gifts for $1.80, $4, and $8.90. Dolla found gifts for $10, $14, and $22. The girls averaged the six prices to get one gift.

   a. About how much did they spend? _____

   b. Explain the steps you took to find the average.

   _____

5. For a science experiment, Sarna mixed baking soda and vinegar to produce gas bubbles. Use the chart to answer the following questions.

Trial 1	140 mg baking soda, 99 mL vinegar
Trial 2	202 mg baking soda, 120 mL vinegar
Trial 3	160 mg baking soda, 140 mL vinegar

   a. How much more baking soda and vinegar did Sarna use in Trial 2 than in Trial 1?

   _____ mg baking soda   _____ mL vinegar

   b. What is the average amount of baking soda and vinegar Sarna used for all three trials?

   _____ mg baking soda   _____ mL vinegar

7-10 CUMULATIVE REVIEW

1. The Sound Shack is having a sale on all CDs. Bud selects five CDs that are marked $9.99, $11.29, $8.79, $5.49, and $13.99.

   a. Round the numbers to the nearest dollar.

   _____ _____ _____ _____ _____

   b. Estimate Bud's total cost. _____

2. Bud's favorite musical group will play one concert at each of the three stadiums near his town. One stadium holds 23,555 people, another holds 17,980 people, and the third holds 38,200 people. If every ticket is sold, about how many people will attend the concert? Round your answer to the nearest thousand.

   _____

Use the chart to answer the questions that follow.

	Stadium 1	Stadium 2	Stadium 3
Category A (lawn seats)	$11.99	$9.75	$17.50
Category B (balcony seats)	$16	$14	$19
Category C (ground floor)	$27.25	$24.95	$28.25

3. Bud and his two friends waited so long to buy tickets at Stadium 2 that they were not able to sit together. They had to buy one ticket from each of the three categories. To the nearest dollar, what was the total cost for all three tickets?

   _____

4. Bud and his friends chose Stadium 2 because the tickets were the cheapest. About how much more are tickets at Stadium 1 than at Stadium 2? Estimate the difference to the nearest dollar.

   Category A _____   Category B _____   Category C _____

5. About how much more are tickets at Stadium 3 than at Stadium 2? Estimate the difference to the nearest dollar.

   Category A _____   Category B _____   Category C _____

11-15 CUMULATIVE REVIEW

Use mental math and the properties of multiplication to find the products.

1. 2×36 _____

2. 19×6 _____

3. 5×32 _____

4. 8×51 _____

5. 27×4 _____

6. 3×29 _____

Solve each problem.

7. Georg and Greta took a bicycle trip from their home in Frankfurt, Germany, to a camping site. The trip was 240.3 kilometers each way. The bikers rode 62 kilometers a day. About how many days did the trip take each way?

_____

8. Georg and Greta packed powdered soup mix to eat. Each packet contained 2.2 servings. Throughout the trip, Georg and Greta used 11.5 packets. About how many servings in all did they eat?

_____

9. Meosha goes to the public library in her town. She finds the section on Japanese history, but she cannot decide which book she wants. The library has four shelves of books on this subject. Each shelf holds about 43 books. About how many books could Meosha read on this subject if she wanted to read everything the library owned on Japanese history?

_____

10. Meosha checks out one book on Japanese history that has 346 pages. She can have the book for two weeks before she will receive an overdue fine. About how many pages a day will she need to read to finish the book before it is overdue?

_____

Estimate each answer below.

1. $\frac{3}{8} + \frac{2}{5}$ _____

2. $\frac{7}{8} - \frac{1}{4}$ _____

3. $2\frac{1}{2} + 2\frac{3}{4}$ _____

4. $8\frac{1}{3} - 6\frac{1}{2}$ _____

5. $1\frac{5}{6} - \frac{1}{5}$ _____

6. $\frac{1}{4} + \frac{1}{2} + \frac{3}{8}$ _____

7. $5\frac{1}{3} \times 2\frac{1}{4}$ _____

8. $9\frac{1}{3} \times \frac{3}{4}$ _____

Duke's skateboard is brand new. He rides it to work, school, parties, and anywhere else he wants to go. Use the chart below to answer the following questions.

Sunday		Monday	
Destination	**Distance Traveled**	**Destination**	**Distance Traveled**
park	$\frac{1}{2}$ mile	park	$1\frac{1}{2}$ mile
Rita's	$\frac{3}{4}$ mile	Rita's	$1\frac{3}{4}$ mile
movies	$\frac{1}{4}$ mile	movies	$\frac{1}{4}$ mile
work	1 mile	work	$1\frac{1}{4}$ mile

9. Duke rides his skateboard everywhere he goes. Estimate how many miles Duke rode on Monday. _____

10. Estimate how many miles Duke rode on Sunday. _____

11. Estimate the difference between the distance from work to Duke's house and from the movie theater to Duke's house. _____

12. Duke rides one mile in about $7\frac{1}{2}$ minutes. About how long will it take him to ride to work and back? _____

Estimate each area below.

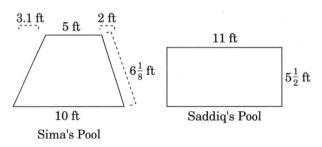

13. Estimate the area of Sima's pool. _____

14. Estimate the area of Saddiq's pool. _____

Estimate each answer.

1. Bernadette's father planned to sew a bouclé dress for Bernadette's school dance. He cut 3 square yards of material on the sewing table. Bernadette's dog jumped on the sewing table and his muddy paws ruined about 0.8 square yard of the material. Estimate the percent of the material that was soiled.

   _____

2. Bernadette's father cut new material and finally finished the knee-length dress. He wanted to use more of the material to make dresses for his other two daughters. He used one quarter of the total amount of material for Bernadette's dress. What percent of material is left for the other two dresses?

   _____

3. Patrick takes a tap-dancing class after school. There are 21 tappers in his class. Patrick and one other person have never taken a tap-dancing class before. Estimate the percent of people in the class who are first-time tappers.

   _____

4. About 19 percent of the 21 tappers in Patrick's class also take ballet class. Estimate how many people are taking both tap dance and ballet.

   _____

5. With her American History class, Danit takes a trip to the Badlands in South Dakota to see Mount Rushmore. The trip will last four nights and five days. There are 11 people in Danit's class. They buy plane tickets for $210 per ticket. They will pay $48 per night to stay in a hotel. They estimate spending about $16 per day for food. About how much will the trip cost per person?

   _____

6. Danit's class took a day trip from Mount Rushmore and drove to another monument, Crazy Horse. The gas for the trip cost about $37, the snacks along the way cost about $13, and the class purchased one professional photograph in front of the monument for $11. About how much did the day trip cost Danit's class?

   _____

ANSWER KEY

LESSON 1 (pp. 2–3)

  1. a. yes **b.** An exact amount is required.

  3. exact value **5.** estimate **7.** exact value

  9. Sample: "What is your budget?"

LESSON 2 (pp. 4–5)

  1. a. 6 **b.** 3 **c.** less than 5 **d.** 860

  3. 500 **5.** 17,000 **7.** 570,000

LESSON 3 (pp. 6–7)

  1. a. 47, 23 **b.** 70

    c. $(70 + 20) - 1 = 90 - 1 = 89$ **d.** 89

  3. 15 **5.** 100 **7.** 34 **9.** 232

  11. a. yes **b.** Because 99 is less than 108.

    c. No. The rounded sums are less than 108.

LESSON 4 (pp. 8–9)

  1. a. 30,000,000 **b.** 60,000,000

    c. 90,000,000

  3. 1,100 **5.** 180 **7.** 35,000 **9.** 22,000

  11. 90,000

LESSON 5 (pp. 10–11)

  1. a. 1960: 3,550,404; 3,600,000

    1990: 2,783,726; 2,800,000

    b. difference: 800,000

  3. 300 **5.** 1,200 **7.** 22,000 **9.** 670,000

  11. a **13.** 40,000,000

LESSON 6 (pp. 12–13)

  1. a. 10, 20, 30 **b.** 60 **c.** 60, 20 **d.** 20

  3. 70 **5.** 700 **7.** 80 **9.** 400

  11. 20,000; 20,010

LESSON 7 (pp. 14–15)

  1. a. 8 is underlined **b.** 5 is circled

    c. equal to **d.** 3.39

  3. 78.09 **5.** $14.60 **7.** $.85 **9.** $.80

  11. 2.15 **13.** 3 **15.** 0.00004

LESSON 8 (pp. 16–17)

  1. a. 1,122; 952; 1,186 **b.** 3,260 **c.** 3,260 mi

  3. $123.6 + 305.4 + 786.1 = 1,215.1$

  5. $14 + 67 + 26 = 107$

  7. $2,153 + 3,959 = 6,112$

  9. $120 + 310 + 790 = 1,220$

  11. Check students' work.

LESSON 9 (pp. 18–19)

  1. a. 4, 4, 4, 5, 6, 6, 5, 5, 6

    b. $4 + 6, 4 + 6, 4 + 6, 5 + 5$ **c.** 45

    d. Sample: Yes, because her total score is 45.

  3. 43; 43.2 **5.** 52; 51.41 **7.** 5,000; 5,072

  9. Sample: 90, 110, 85, 48, 150, 51, 47, 98, 1, 0

LESSON 10 (pp. 20–21)

  1. a. $.80 **b.** Sample: $1.00 − $.80 is easier

    than $1.00 − $.77. **c.** $.20

  3. $21 - 8 = 13$ **5.** $6 - 1 = 5$

  7. $33 - 13 = 20$ **9.** $39 - 29 = 10$

  11. $13 - 5 = 8$ **13.** 5.96 seconds; $61 - 55 = 6$

LESSON 11 (pp. 22–23)

  1. a. 4 and 8 **b.** 32 **c.** 3 **d.** 32,000

  3. 1,500 **5.** 260 **7.** 140 **9.** 550 **11.** 420

LESSON 12 (pp. 24–25)

  1. a. 100, 60 **b.** $100 \times 60 = 6,000$ **c.** 6,000

  3. $30 \times 70 = 2,100$

  5. $500 \times 70 = 35,000$

LESSON 13 (pp. 26–27)

  1. a. $2,000 \div 60$

    b. Samples: $2,000 \div 50$ or $1,800 \div 60$.

    c. Samples: $2,000 \div 50 = 40$

    or $1,800 \div 60 = 30$

  3. $600 \div 75 = 8$; $581 \div 72 = 8.1$

  5. $600 \div 30 = 20$; $625 \div 27 = 23.1$

  7. $6,000 \div 75 = 80$; $5,780 \div 74 = 78.1$

  9. $18,000 \div 60 = 300$; $17,381 \div 64 = 271.6$

  11. $12,000 \div 30 = 400$; $11,850 \div 34 = 348.5$

    or 349

LESSON 14 (pp. 28–29)

1. **a.** 0.8, 20   **b.** $0.8 \times 20 = 16$ **c.** 16
3. 6×7; 42   5. 30×7; 210
7. $20 \times 6 = 120$, which is an overestimate. The display is incorrect; $12.9 \times 7.4 = 74.562$

LESSON 15 (pp. 30–31)

1. **a.** $78.60 \div 12 = ?$ **b.** $80 \div 12$ **c.** $80 \div 10$
   d. About $8.
   Answers may vary for exercises 2–10
3. $480 \div 6 = 80$ 5. $270 \div 3 = 90$
7. $3,200 \div 8 = 400$ 9. $5,400 \div 90 = 60$
11. **a.** $44 \div 4 = 11$ **b.** Sample: A compatible number for 45.19 could be 44; divided by 4 runners
13. **a.** $700 \div 20 = \$35$ **b.** Sample: A compatible number for 714.25 could be 720; divided by 18

LESSON 16 (pp. 32–33)

1. **a.** $\frac{1}{2}$ yd, $\frac{1}{2}$ yd   **b.** $\frac{1}{2} + \frac{1}{2} = 1$
   c. $\frac{4}{9} + \frac{11}{18} = 1\frac{1}{18}$ yd or $0.444 + 0.611 = 1.055$ yd   **d.** Yes; 1 is close to $1\frac{1}{18}$ or 1.055
3. $0 + 1 = 1$ 5. $\frac{1}{2} + 0 + 1 = 1\frac{1}{2}$
7. $1 + 1 + 0 = 2$ 9. $1 + 0 + 1 = 2$
11. **a–d.** Answers will vary.   **e.** The sum represents the fraction of each weekday that you sleep, are in school, or work.

LESSON 17 (pp. 34–35)

1. **a.** 6 ft   **b.** 5 ft   **c.** $6 + 5 + 6 + 5 = 22$ ft
   d. $21\frac{7}{8}$ ft or 21.875 ft   **e.** yes; 22 ft is close to the actual sum.
3. $3\frac{1}{2} + 5 + 9\frac{1}{2} = 18$
5. $6 + 4 + 9 + 2\frac{1}{2} = 21\frac{1}{2}$
7. $5 + 6 + 8 + 3 = 22$

LESSON 18 (pp. 36–37)

1. **a.** $13\frac{1}{2}$ oz, 27 oz   **b.** $27 - 13\frac{1}{2} = ?$
   c. $26\frac{2}{2} - 13\frac{1}{2} = 13\frac{1}{2}$ **d.** $13\frac{1}{2}$ oz
   e. $13\frac{11}{24}$ oz or 13.458 oz
   f. yes; $13\frac{1}{2}$ is close to 13.46.
3. $7 - 5 = 2$ 5. $11\frac{1}{2} - 1 = 10\frac{1}{2}$
7. $8\frac{1}{2} - 8 = \frac{1}{2}$

LESSON 19 (pp. 38–39)

1. **a.** $\frac{1}{2} \times 1\frac{2}{3}$ **b.** 2   **c.** $\frac{1}{2} \times 2 = 1$ **d.** $\frac{5}{6}$
   e. Yes, they are close.
3. $\frac{1}{2}, \frac{7}{12}$ 5. 6   7. 24   9. 45
11. Answers may vary. Sample: $8\frac{1}{4}$ rounds to 8 and $\frac{1}{2}$ of 8 is 4.

LESSON 20 (pp. 40–41)

1. **a.** $A = l \times w$ **b.** 10.5 m by 4.2 m
   c. 11 m by 4 m   **d.** 44 square meters
3. 144 sq yd; $152\frac{1}{9}$ sq yd   5. 24 sq ft

LESSON 21 (pp. 42–43)

1. **a.** parallelogram and triangle
   b. 50,000 square miles
   c. 15,000 square miles
   d. 65,000 square miles
3. 48 square miles   5. 140 square meters

LESSON 22 (pp. 44–45)

1. **a.** 4   **b.** $\frac{1}{4}$ **c.** $\frac{1}{4} = \frac{25}{100} = 25\%$
3. 25%   5. 70%   7. 44%
9. Answers will vary.

LESSON 23 (pp. 46–47)

1. **a.** $11\% \times 195 = ?$ **b.** $\frac{1}{10}$ **c.** 200
d. about 20 students **e.** 21.45; yes, it's close.

3–7. Answers may vary.
3. $\frac{1}{4} \times 100 = 25$ 5. $\frac{1}{2} \times 50 = 25$
7. $\frac{1}{3} \times 60 = 20$ 9. about 200 students

LESSON 24 (pp. 48–49)

1. **a.** $\frac{19}{49}$ **b.** $\frac{20}{50}$ **c.** $\frac{40}{100}$ **d.** 40%
e. 38.8%; they are close
3. $\frac{25}{100}$ or 25% 5. $\frac{4}{5}$ or 80% 7. $\frac{1}{2}$ or 50%
9. $\frac{25}{100}$ or 25%
11. about 20%

LESSON 25 (pp. 50–51)

1. **a.** $5 **b.** $15; $3 **c.** $7
d. Cheryl; she spends about $5 and Neil spends about $7 **e.** Sample answer: You have to compare like units.
3. Estimate may vary. 3. $80

CUMULATIVE REVIEW (L1–L3) (p. 52)

1. **a.** estimate **b.** exact
3. **a.** estimate for meal calories: 1,000 calories
b. estimate for difference: 40 calories actual difference: 90 calories

CUMULATIVE REVIEW (L4–L6) (p. 53)

1. $28,500
3. 1st quarter: 12; 2nd quarter: 25; 3rd quarter: 45; 4th quarter: 58.5
5. **a.** 60 mg baking soda, 20 mL vinegar
b. 170 mg baking soda, 120 mL vinegar

CUMULATIVE REVIEW (L7–L10) (p. 54)

1. **a.** $10, $11, $9, $5, $14 **b.** $49
3. $49 5. $8; $5; $3

CUMULATIVE REVIEW (L11–L15) (p. 55)

1. 72 3. 160 5. 108 7. about 4 days
9. about 160 books

CUMULATIVE REVIEW (L16–L21) (p. 56)

1. 1 3. $5\frac{1}{2}$ 5. $1\frac{1}{2}$ 7. 10 9. 5 miles
11. $\frac{1}{2}$ mile 13. 45 square feet

CUMULATIVE REVIEW (L22–L25) (p. 57)

1. 33% 3. 10% 5. $500